Cougars! Amazing Fact for Kids (Picture Book)

All information in this book has been carefully researched and checked for factual accuracy. However, the author and publisher make no warranty, express or implied, that the information contained herein is appropriate for every individual, situation, or purpose and assume no responsibility for errors or omissions. The reader assumes the risk and full responsibility for all actions, and the author will not be held responsible for any loss or damage, whether consequential, incidental, special, or otherwise, that may result from the information presented in this book.

All images have been purchased from stock photo sites or are royalty-free for commercial use.

I have relied on my own observations as well as many different sources for this book, and I have done my best to check facts and give credit where it is due. In the event that any material is used without proper permission, please contact me so that the oversight can be corrected.

Cougars are also called mountain lions.

They're the fourth-largest cat species.

Cougars can jump 18 feet high.

They live up to 12 years in wild.

Cougars are solitary and territorial.

Their roar sounds like a human scream.

They can run up to 50 mph.

Eat deer, elk, and even insects.

Cougars are excellent climbers.

They live in mountains and forests.

Baby cougars are called cubs.

Cubs have spots that fade with age.

Cougars have a wide habitat range.

They're active mostly at dawn and dusk.

Cougars use stealth to hunt.

They cover uneaten food with leaves.

Can leap 40 feet horizontally.

Cougars have a lifespan of 8-13 years.

They do not roar like other big cats.

Cougars have about 50 teeth.

Mostly silent, communicate with visuals.

Excellent swimmers but prefer land.

They avoid humans and other cougars.

Tail helps with balance and sharp turns.

Mothers teach cubs to hunt at 6 months.

Can consume up to 10 pounds of meat daily.

Cougars are very adaptable to environments.

Rarely seen in the wild by humans.

Their eyes glow in the dark.

Cougars are ambush predators.

They have whiskers for sensing close objects.

Cubs' mortality rate is high in wild.

Protect livestock by keeping animals secure.

Cougars maintain ecological balance.

Rarely attack humans, prefer avoiding conflict.

Cougars can purr like domestic cats.

Solitary except during mating or motherhood.

They mark territory with scent marks.

Highly skilled in navigation and memory.

Cougars are an umbrella species for conservation.

Made in United States
North Haven, CT
30 November 2024

61259988R00024